I0624453

BIG MIKE'S

BAJAN COOKING

MIKE SPRINGER

Big Mike's Bajan Cooking

Copyright © Sept 2024 by Mike Springer

ISBN: 978-1-958356-42-5

All rights reserved. No part of this publication may be reproduced, stored in retrieval system, copied in any form or by any means, electronic, mechanical, photocopying, recording or otherwise transmitted without written permission from the copyright owner. You must not circulate this book in any format.

This e-book may not be re-sold or given away to other people. If you would like to share this book with another person, please purchase an additional copy for each recipient.
www.chefbigmikes.com

Published by: TAWCarlisle Publishing

CONTENTS

INTRODUCTION

Bajans (Barbadians) love nothing more than a never ending buffet. A cacophony of tastes that we can savour...

I am Big Mike from Big Mike's Calypso kitchen, A "Bajan Limey" born and raised in England until 11 years old, then until 18 years old I lived in sunny Barbados, 'the land of the flying fish' where I explored food and authentic flavours of traditional dishes and some I discovered and developed myself.

I am Anglo Bajan and proud. I am lucky enough to have two homes; Barbados and London, but I have one true love—Bajan Cuisine.

I make food that takes you back to delicious taste explosions you uncovered as a child and that you nurtured to adulthood. I simply adore those sound bites from school dinners over here in "Blighty" growing up and entwined with my "Columbic" culinary exploration of Barbadian seashore delicacies, to my late night slamming of domino quick fix delights that made me label Barbados home.

"Bajan's luv food that much, we even put a fork of the Flag", so let me take you on a journey of Barbadian culinary delights that I enjoy cooking and sharing with my friends.

Big Mike's Rum Shop Gravy; "Great Umami food for those intoxicating times."

I simply love food, drink & life.

So come with me for a "Small taste of Barbados big taste of the Caribbean."

Crossover to my world where all my dreams are delicious and edible.

CALYPSO AVOCADO PINEAPPLE & MANGO SALSA

CALYPSO AVOCADO PINEAPPLE & MANGO SALSA

A delicious Summer salad. It's zingy, it's refreshing, it's crunchy, it's tasty. It can go with virtually anything at any time, especially a great glass of wine or rum punch.

(Serves 4-6)

INGREDIENTS

1 avocado peeled pitted and diced
½ fresh pineapple cored peeled and diced
1 mango peeled pitted and diced
1 bonnet pepper finely diced
1 red bell pepper cored de-seeded and diced
2 tomatoes diced
½ cucumber diced
1 cup of spring onions diced
3 tbsp coriander
2 tbsp flat parsley
6 tbsp lime Juice
3 tbsp olive oil
3 pinches sea salt
2 pinches ground black cracked pepper

INSTRUCTIONS

1. Combine all ingredients in a bowl and stir until mixed.
2. Can be served immediately but I have found for best results cover and refrigerate for about an hour. This allows the infusion of the lime and sea salt throughout your salsa, intensifying the taste. Mmmmmmm.

Tasty Tips

Once you have peeled your avocado, squeeze a smidgen of lime juice over the top to prevent your avocado darkening.

BAJAN STYLED CORNED BEEF (CARIBBEAN)

BAJAN STYLED CORNED BEEF (CARIBBEAN)

This is one of these dishes that always takes' me back home to Barbados and my mum. It's truly a classic, simple dish, that I loved growing up with. So, trust me when I say this goes great with white rice, crackers, and garlic crostinis. It always leads to a great time at my house.

(Serves 4-6)

INGREDIENTS

1can of corned beef 340g (sliced into rectangular patties)
1 bouquet garni of fresh thyme and rosemary
1 medium white onion sliced
1 scotch bonnet pepper
5 tbsp tomato ketchup
2 tbsp light soy
4 tbsp olive oil
5 tbsp hot water

INSTRUCTIONS

1. Heat oil in a frying pan over a moderate heat
2. Add your bouquet garni of fresh thyme and rosemary to the pan
3. Add your corned beef patties in a clockwise motion so that they are equally proportioned across the pan
4. Add your tomatoes and scotch bonnet pepper evenly into the pan.
5. Add onions
6. Add the tomato ketchup and soy evenly into the pan
7. Carefully flip your corn beef patties over with the onion now on the hot side of the pan

8. You will have noticed the corned beef will have caramelized on the top.
9. Finally add your hot water and leave to simmer for 10 to 15 minutes this will allow the onions and tomatoes to caramelize and for your sauce to thicken & gain depth of flavor

Serve hot from the pot

GARLIC AND BUTTER INFUSED CROSTINI

GARLIC AND BUTTER INFUSED CROSTINI

The simple things in life are best.

On its own dipped in hot sauce or eaten with corned beef this little number is niiiice.

(Serves 4-6)

INGREDIENTS

2 ciabatta bread sliced length ways
1 bouquet garni of thyme & rosemary
2 tbsp Salted butter
1 tbsp Olive oil
3 crushed bulbs of garlic

INSTRUCTIONS

1. Warm butter and olive oil in a frying pan over a moderate heat.
2. When the oil is hot add your bouquet garni of thyme and Rosemary.
3. Add your three bulbs of garlic and immediately add your halves of ciabatta into your garlic oil slice side down.
4. Sauté your ciabatta until they go golden brown on one side then turn over and Sauté for approx. 30 seconds or until slightly golden brown.
5. Remove from pan and put onto a grill tray and place into the oven on a moderate heat to crisp up.
6. Look for a slight crisp bite to enhance texture to your meal.
7. Remove from oven and serve either hot or at room temperature.

SMOKED MACKEREL SCOTCH EGGS AND BAJAN HOT SAUCE MAYONNAISE

SMOKED MACKEREL SCOTCH EGGS AND BAJAN HOT SAUCE MAYONNAISE

Simply a scrumptious pescatarian treat not to be missed and goes perfectly with our hot sauce mayonnaise. Oh my word, it's good.

INGREDIENTS

4 smoked macro fillets skinned
4 small eggs
2 tbs of cream cheese
Half a bunch of coriander chopped
Half a bunch of parsley chopped
Half limes zest
100 grams of flour
Half a bonnet pepper chopped finely
 Half a lime, zest only
100 g of flour, that's extra for dusting
2 eggs, beaten
150 g of Panko breadcrumbs
1 tsp of English Mustard
Sea salt

Bajan hot sauce mayonnaise.
4 tablespoons of mayonnaise
1 tablespoon of a good Bajan and hot sauce
1 teaspoon of English mustard
I pinch of sea salt

INSTRUCTIONS

1. Boil the eggs for five minutes, then refresh in ice cold water. Peel and lay on a cloth to dry.

2. Place mackerel, cream cheese, lime zest, coriander and parsley in a food processor and pulse until only just blended - the mix should be nice and coarse.

3. Divide the mix into four and flatten out into round patty shapes similar in dimension to burgers. Dust the eggs through flour, place one on each patty and carefully wrap the mix around the eggs. Place in the fridge to set for approximately one hour.

4. Once set, remove from the fridge and pass each Scotch egg through the flour, egg and breadcrumbs to cook evenly. Set aside until needed.

5. For the Bajan hot sauce mayonnaise. Mix together mayonnaise with the hot sauce a good pinch of sea salt and 1 teaspoon of English mustard.

6. Deep-fried the Scotch eggs for 2 to 3 minutes at 180°C, until golden and crispy. Drain on kitchen paper and season with course sea salt.

7. Serve Scotch eggs warm with the Bajan hot sauce mayonnaise.

FRIED CASSAVA CHIPS

If you love a chip crispy on the outside super fluffy on the inside.
These cassava chips are the cream and queen of all chips.

INGREDIENTS

Fresh or frozen cassava chips
Vegetable oil
Sea Salt
Cayenne pepper
Dried rosemary and thyme

INSTRUCTIONS

1. Peel and chop the cassava in quarters
2. Place in a pot of boiling water and cook the cassava until soft
3. Once cooked remove from the water and leave to dry
4. In a deep skillet or fat fryer add oil and leave until hot.
5. Add for dried cassava and leave to fry until golden brown
6. Once golden-brown remove from oil and place on kitchen paper to absorb the extra oil.
7. Sprinkle sea salt dried thyme and rosemary over chips with a pinch of chilly and serve immediately.

VEGAN FRIED CHICKEN BITES (JACKFRUIT).

VEGAN FRIED CHICKEN BITES (JACKFRUIT).

It looks like fried chicken, it tastes like fried chicken, but it's jackfruit, a fantastic vegan option which really packs a punch of flavour. Liked by vegans, vegetarians and carnivores a like. One of my favourites.

INGREDIENTS

1x 565 g tin of young green jackfruit in brine
Vegetable oil
Parsley
4 tablespoons of soya light

For Seasoning
3 teaspoons of Cajun seasoning
Half a teaspoon of smoked paprika
Half a teaspoon of onion powder
Half a teaspoon of garlic powder
Half a teaspoon of black pepper

For Coating
60 grams of plain flour
60 g of arrow root starch
Half a teaspoon of ground black pepper
Half a teaspoon of salt

INSTRUCTIONS

1. Drain and rinse Jackfruit and put into a pot of boiling water and cook until tender, for 20 to 30 mins.
2. Drain and dry on kitchen plate until cooled.
3. Slice each piece into bite-size chunks and trim for hard-core ends. Then add to a mixing bowl, along with all the ingredients for the seasoning and stir until fully combined. Put seasoned jackfruit into the fridge preferably overnight, but for a minimum of 2 hours.
4. Meanwhile, combine three coating ingredients in a separate mixing bowl and set aside. Add the jackfruit into the mixing flour and coat evenly.
5. Add oil into frying pan or a fat fryer and ensure it is hot. You can ensure the oil is hot by testing with a sprinkle of flour. Place coated Jackfruit into fryer until golden brown then place on a kitchen towel to soak up any excess oil.
6. Serve with vegan mayonnaise or a dip of your choice.

SALT CRUSTED BAKED SALMON

SALT CRUSTED BAKED SALMON

This dish is fit for any Banquet. or Special Occasion. A great centre piece with explosive flavours.

INGREDIENTS

1X2.5 kg whole salmon gutted girls remove scales left on
4 lemons
4 limes
2 oranges
1 bulb of fennel
2 x large onions (finely chopped)
Half a bunch of fresh flat leaf parsley (15 G)
Half a bunch of fresh coriander (15 g)
Fresh thyme (7 g)
Fresh rosemary (7g)
5 kg of kosher salt
Half a bunch of fresh basil

INSTRUCTIONS

1. Preheat the oven to 180° C/350°F
2. Wash the salmon well both inside and out then Pat dry with kitchen paper
3. Sprinkle two pinches of salt into the cavity of the salmon
4. Finely slice lemons limes orange & fennel & stuff into the cavity of salmon along with fresh herbs chives and onions.
5. Combined rock salt with 250 ml of water in a large bowl to form a snow like texture.

6. Spread one third of the mixture over a large baking tray to ensure the salmon sits on the salt

7. Make a slight hole in the middle to hold the salmon snuggly, lay salmon diagonally in the tray, then spoon over the remaining salt mixture, putting it around and on top the salmon to create an even 2 cm thick layer all over the fish.

8. Bake for 45 minutes

9. To test the salmon is ready, push a skewer through the salt into the thickest part of the fish, if it comes out warm after five seconds, it's done. Remove from the oven and set aside in the crust for just one hour.

   Lightly crack the salt casing and pull it away from the salmon, brushing any excess from the top and gently loosen. Pull the skin away, leaving you with a beautifully cooked pink salmon which you can rustically remove in flakes.

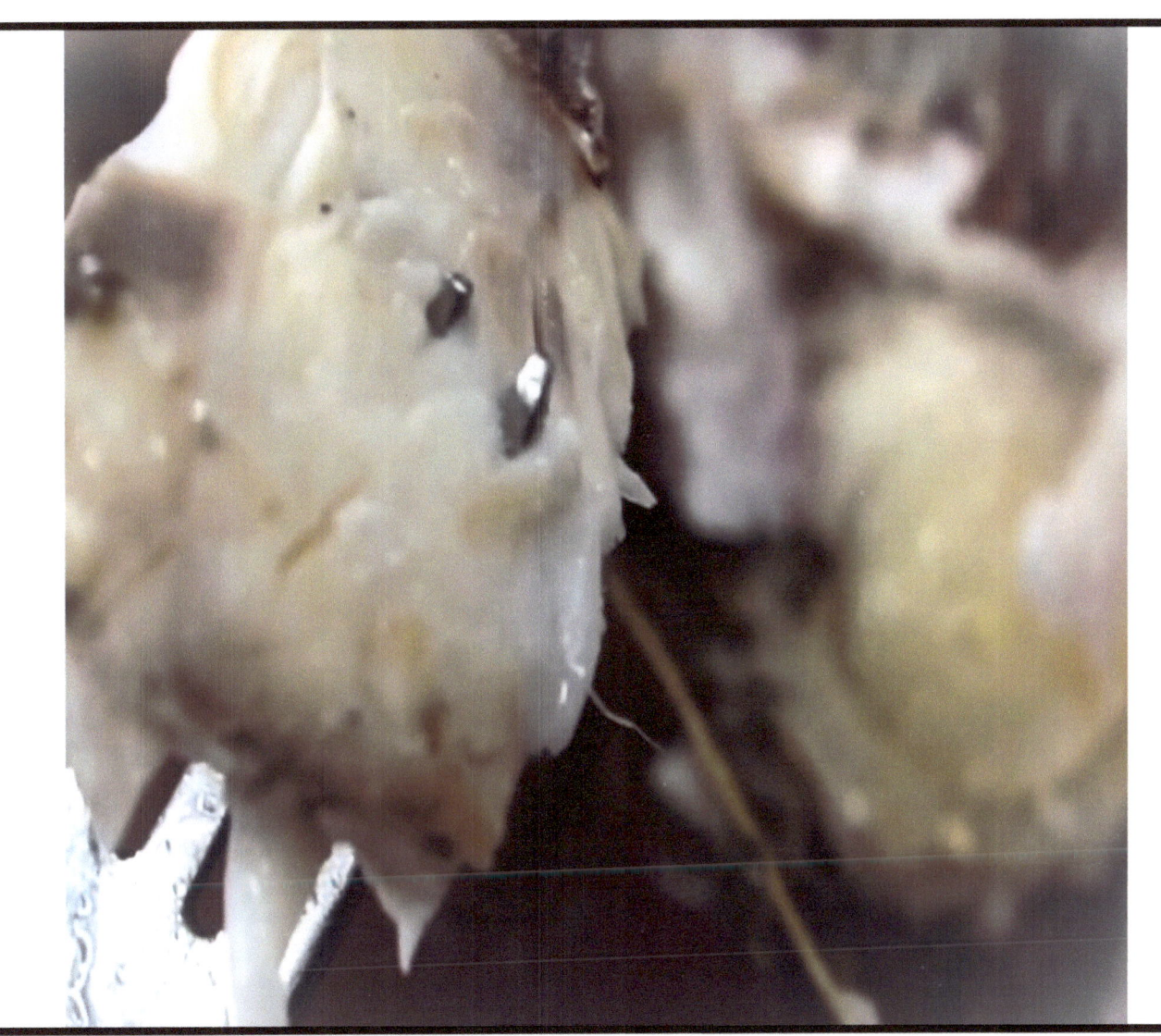

CALYPSO ROASTED SEA BASS

CARIBBEAN GRILLED WHOLE SEA BASS

Caribbean Grilled Whole Sea Bass- Fairly Easy to make with a great blend of spice - moist, tender and delicious.

INGREDIENTS

1- 2 whole Sea Bass about 1- 1 1/2 kg each
1-2 fresh lemons
salt to taste
1 tsp ground white pepper
1 tsp ground all spice
1 tbs garlic cloves minced
1 tsp ginger minced
1 tsp paprika
2 tsp thyme finely chopped
½ cup basil or parsley coarsely chopped

INSTRUCTIONS

1. Make three – four diagonal cuts in each side of the fish, all the way right through the bone. Season fish with salt, pepper, and squeeze some lemon over it. Set aside
2. In a small bowl mix all the ingredients to make marinade for fish.
3. Pour the marinade over the fish, and gently flip them back and forth until coated inside and out. Let it marinate in the fridge for up to 24hours
4. Preheat to grill to a medium heat and baste your fish with some extra marinade.
5. When you are ready, grill the fish for about 3- 4 minutes you may have to add a minute on two depending on the thickness of your fish.

JERK CHICKEN

JERK CHICKEN

Jerk Chicken or Peppered chicken is classic through out the cariibbean. This is my Bajan twist on this dish. Taste great in the oven or on the charcoal BBQ.

INGREDIENTS

12 chicken thighs, bone in
1 lime

For the marinade
1 big bunch spring onions , roughly chopped
Thumb-sized ginger, roughly chopped
3 garlic cloves
½ a small onion
3 scotch bonnet peppers , deseeded if you want less heat
½ tsp dried , or 1 tbsp thyme leaves
1 lime juiced
2 tbsp soy sauce
2 tbsp vegetable oil
3 tbsp brown sugar
1 tbsp ground allspice

INSTRUCTIONS

1. To make the jerk marinade, combine the ingredients in a food processor along with 1 tsp salt, and blend to a purée. If you're having trouble getting it to blend, just keep turning off the blender, stirring the mixture, and trying again. Eventually it will start to blend up – don't be tempted to add water, as you want a thick paste.

2. Make a few slashes in 12 chicken thighs and pour the marinade over the chicken, rubbing it into all the crevices. Cover and leave to marinate overnight in the fridge.

3. If you want to barbecue your chicken, get the coals burning 1 hr. or so before you're ready to cook. Authentic jerk chicken is charcoal smoke-grilled. To get a more authentic jerk experience, add some rum soaked wood chips to your barbecue, and cook your chicken over slow, indirect heat for 30 mins.

4. To cook in the oven, heat to 180C/160C fan/gas 4. Put the chicken pieces in a roasting tin with the halved lime and cook for 45 mins until tender and cooked through.

MAC CHEESE BALLS

MAC CHEESE BALLS

Mac Cheese or a we Bajans would say "MAC PIE" is national institution.
We eat Mac Pie at every opportunity event & gathering.

So Mac Cheese Balls are a proud tribute to Bajan Mac Pie.
Anytime Anyplace Anytime!

(Makes 25 balls)

INGREDIENTS

5 cups macaroni (500 g)
2 tablespoons butter
2 teaspoons flour
1 ¾ cups milk (400 mL)
2 ½ cups cheddar cheese (250 g)
2 ½ cups red Leicester (250 g)
Salt, to taste
Pepper, to taste
2 eggs, for egg wash
Panko breadcrumbs

INSTRUCTIONS

1. Boil water, add macaroni and cook until al dente
2. Melt butter in a pan and mix 2 tsp flour into it.
3. Add the milk gradually.
4. Add both cheeses and cook until melted and the sauce is thick
5. Season with salt and pepper.
6. Add the cooked macaroni and thoroughly cover.
7. Refrigerate mixture for one hour.

8. Take mixture out and form into balls on another plate.
9. Refrigerate for 2 hours.
10. Dip the solid balls in egg wash, then breadcrumbs.
11. Fry in hot pan of oil until golden brown on both sides.

CARAMEL CHEESE CAKE CRUNCH

CARAMEL CHEESE CAKE CRUNCH

My favorite desserts are Sticky Toffee Pudding Cheese Cake & Apple Crumble

When on offer I can never make up my mind which one; So I decided to create my very own Caramel Cheese Cake Crunch my new favorite.

INGREDIENTS

Cookie Crust
80 g digestive cookie crumbs
40 g melted butter unsalted
1/8 teaspoon cinnamon
1 tablespoon brown sugar

Cheesecake Filling
300 g cream cheese room temperature
70 g granulated sugar
35 g lemon juice freshly squeezed
2 medium eggs room temperature
1/2 teaspoon vanilla extract

Apple Crumble Topping
2 medium granny smith apples peeled and diced
30 g granulated sugar
Pinch of nutmeg
¼ teaspoon cinnamon
45 g all-purpose flour (self raising)

30 g rolled oats
60 g unsalted butter room temperature
60 g brown sugar

Salted Caramel Sauce
150 g caster sugar
40 g water
120 g heavy cream
1/2 teaspoon salt

INSTRUCTIONS

Preheat your fan oven to 150°C (300°F) or 165°C if you're not using a fan oven. Line the bottom of a 18 cm (7 inch) springform pan with baking paper. Set aside.

1. Using a food processor ground your cookies. In a separate bowl, combine them with melted butter, cinnamon and granulated sugar using a spoon. Press the mixture into the bottom of the pan. Bake for 5-6 minutes then set aside to cool.
2. In a large bowl, using a hand mixer, mix together the cream cheese, sugar, vanilla extract and lemon juice until combined and smooth. Add one egg at the time, scraping the sides of the bowl to make sure everything is thoroughly combined. Set aside while you prepare the topping.
3. Peel and dice apples. You should have around 130 g of diced apple. If you put too much, the filling might not support the topping. In a small bowl, combine apples with sugar, cinnamon and nutmeg.
4. Make streusel topping by mixing together all-purpose flour, rolled oats, unsalted butter and sugar. Squeezing it with your hands, you should be able to form small clumps to scatter over apples.
5. Pour the filling over a cooled and baked cookie crust. Smooth it out with a small offset spatula. Sprinkle with prepared apples, then with streusel topping. You might not need all of it. Bake for 25-30 minutes in a preheated oven.
6. Once it's done, place the pan on a cooling rack and leave it to cool to room temperature. Then put the cheesecake in the fridge to cool completely, at least 4 hours.
7. Before serving, generously drizzle over caramel sauce. Enjoy!

Salted Caramel Sauce

1. In a thick bottom saucepan combine sugar and water. Make sure every sugar granule is covered with water. Heat it up over medium to high heat, until it reaches golden amber colour. DO NOT STIR IT. This will take about 15 minutes.

2. While the sugar is dissolving, heat the heavy cream to a simmer. Once the sugar syrup reaches a desired colour, pour the heavy cream over it in a steady stream, stirring constantly with a silicone spatula. There will be a lot of bubbles and steam, be careful not to burn yourself.

3. Once all the bubbles have subsided, put the saucepan back on the stove and cook it for 1-2 minutes, stirring constantly. When it's done, put the caramel sauce in a clean jar and leave it to cool to room temperature.

COCONUT SWEET BREAD

COCONUT SWEET BREAD

My mother's recipe: This is Barbados National Dessert best served with everything. Its golden it rich with sugar spices & the aroma is unmistakeable.

Mum, thank you.

INGREDIENTS

1 ½ cup self-raising flour
1 ½ tsp baking powder
500g Butter (salted)
1 ¼ cup grated coconut
½ cup sugar
¼ cup cherries, finely chopped
¼ cup mixed citrus peel, finely chopped
¼ tsp cinnamon
1 egg
½ tsp pure vanilla extract
1/3 cup milk
½ cup raisins

INSTRUCTIONS

1. Preheat oven to 325 degrees.
2. Add flour and baking powder to a small bowl.
3. Add butter, coconut, sugar, cherries, citrus peel, raisins and cinnamon and mix well.
4. Combine egg, vanilla and milk in a small bowl and whisk to combine. Add to dry ingredients and mix until well incorporated.
5. Pour batter into a greased pan lined with parchment paper and place into preheated oven and bake for 50 minutes to 1 hour.

6. In a small bowl combine 1 tbsp of sugar and 1 tbsp of water and brush over the top. Return to oven for 3-4 minutes.

PAN FRIED FILLETS OF RED SNAPPER SERVED WITH SAMPHIRE GINGER STIR FRIED EGG NOODLES.

PAN FRIED FILLETS OF RED SNAPPER SERVED WITH SAMPHIRE GINGER STIR FRIED EGG NOODLES.

So tasty rather healthy my go too feel good meal

(Serves 4)
INGREDIENTS

Samphire washed & coarsely chopped
Large white onion finely chopped
Bulbs of garlic crushed
Bouquet Garni of Fresh Thyme & Rosemary
Ginger finely sliced
Chinese Chili
Olive Oil
Good quality Egg Noodles
Salt for seasoning

Red Snapper
4 Fillets of red snapper (skin on de-boned and de-scaled)
2 tbsp Jerk Seasoning
6 tbsp Lime Juice
2 tbsp Light Soya
3 tbsp Soya
1Bouquet Garni of Fresh Thyme & Rosemary

Stir Fry

INSTRUCTIONS

Red Snapper
1. Wash fillets of fish & pat dry
2. *Place fillets into a bowl and add jerk seasoning soya lime juice & marinate for 6 hrs. (or overnight for the best tasting results) cover and place in fridge*
3. Remove from fridge 1hr before frying
4. Heat oil in pan and place fish skin side down
5. Fry until skin has golden caramelisation and crispy
6. Flip fillets and turn off the heat and leave the fish to cook in the residual heat for 1-2 minutes. This will ensure fish is moist & flaky
7. Remove fish from oil onto a tissue/cloth to soak up excess oil.

Stir Fry

1. Cook egg noodles in hot water drain & drizzle a tbsp of olive oil Put aside
2. Heat oil in fry pan and add Bari onions garlic ginger add onions. Fry your onions and begin to soften (Be careful not to burn the garlic)
3. Add Samphire and stir fry for 1-2 mins (We want Samphire to have a bite).
4. Add chili and soya and stir fry then your egg noodles in 4 parts.
5. Carefully combine all ingredients together and ensure an even blend of noodles and mixture throughout.

Serve immediately with fish

SOCIAL LINKS

Visit Mike's website at www.chefbigmikes.com

Great Britain's Takeaway Chef of the year 2016 (finalist 2018 and 19)
https://youtu.be/TfLQpu0ZTpY

The Dancing Chef of The X Factor (chef factor) adverts 2017
https://youtu.be/W0A7FOJFOdY

Part of the Made you look Exhibition. Top Black Chefs in the UK.
https://www.boxpark.co.uk/blog/exhibition-made-you-look-by-julian-george/

DESCRIPTION

Small taste of Barbados big taste of the Caribbean.

Whether you are from the Caribbean or just want to try out great food from Barbados, Big Mike's Bajan Cooking will provide the very best selection of Bajan authentic recipes that will inspire you.

Mike Springer's incredible home-cooked meals created a stir, and he became widely known after winning the British Takeaway Awards and appearing on X-factor as the dancing chef.

You will be tempted by a selection of recipes such as; tasty Vegan Fried Chicken, succulent Salt Crusted Baked Salmon and flavoursome Jerk Chicken.

This essential guide will take you to Barbados with delicious easy-to-follow recipes that you will love.

Impress your family and friends with amazing new dishes from the Caribbean, download your copy today!

www.ingramcontent.com/pod-product-compliance
Lightning Source LLC
Chambersburg PA
CBHW041555120626
46551CB00002B/218